DAILY ENCOUNTER WITH JESUS

Daily devotions that draw you closer to God for a victorious life

Morning and evening manna for you and your family

ADAH NYINOMUJUNI

authorHOUSE®

AuthorHouse™
1663 Liberty Drive
Bloomington, IN 47403
www.authorhouse.com
Phone: 1-800-839-8640

First published by AuthorHouse   08/29/2011

ISBN: 978-1-4567-9670-9 (sc)
ISBN: 978-1-4567-9671-6 (ebk)

Printed in the United States of America

DAILY
ENCOUNTER WITH
JESUS

Dedication

This book is dedicated to the leadership of Bethel International Tabernacle. I so appreciate their great support to me in serving God's people.

Acknowledgement

I would like to give special thanks to Joyce Nangai who financially stood with me to have this manuscript in print. Special thanks to Emmanuel Nkukumila for his advice and encouragement in doing this work. A big, 'Thank You' to all those who encouraged me to write these devotions. There may be others who indirectly contributed to make this manuscript a success whose names do not appear here. May the Good Lord shower abundant graces and blessings upon them.

Preface

I really honor you for picking up this book. Actually in doing so you have made a decision to live more deliberately, more joyfully and completely for that is the step ahead in quest for God in your life. You have indeed decided to live your life by choice rather than by chance, buy design rather than by default. Hence for this I thank you so much.

My deepest desire for you is to come closer to God through the different powerful and moving reflections contained in this book; that will bring abundance of God's grace to your life and that of others who come your way.

I was moved to write these devotions because of the question I have heard often asked, "How do I read the Bible?" I don't know how to go about it, many people say. I see great hunger manifesting itself in lots of people I meet every day; it is not a physical hunger for food, but one for spiritual food—the word of God. However, I am convinced that praying for these hungry souls is not enough; hence I feel the call within me to act on the word of the Lord Jesus Christ that He spoke to the apostle Peter *"Simon, son of John, do you love me more than these? . . . . "Feed my lambs . . . "Tend my sheep" . . . "Feed my sheep . . ." John 21:15-17.*

It is apodictic that many writers written devotional books and have tried to help many people come closer to God. However, the spiritual needs of the billions of people around the world seem more than what these books can contain. Hence, I developed the impetus to write this devotional book to contribute to the mission of helping people come closer to God in their lives.

The daily devotions in this book have been written in a very simple and effective way to enable every reader to grasp, reflect on and act upon the message contained in here. Nevertheless, every reader is encouraged to read these devotions carefully and prayerfully. In addition, the scriptural references for the articles have to meditated upon after which the article should be read.

Furthermore, after reading, take time to pray and ask the Lord to plant the word in your heart so you can walk in the light of the word throughout the day.

At the end of each week take time to meditate on the devotions you have been reading throughout the week in order to measure your progress in your daily walk with Christ. Ask yourself if these devotions are transforming your life in any way. Indeed, they will because the word of God on John 6: 63, *"It is the spirit that gives life, the fresh is of no avail; the words that I have spoken to you are spirit and life."*

Introduction

This Daily Encounter With Jesus comes to you packed with soul stirring thoughts that will feed your spirit man and give you strength and direction for each day. It is a powerful spiritual book containing daily morning and evening devotions that will lift, transform and enhance your spiritual life. These devotions have been written with relevant and most suitable biblical references to guide you on how to go about your daily affairs in a godly way that will lead you and others around you to a victorious kind of life. This is because at the end of every biblical reference, I have presented practical ways that surely will help you live your life in a right and admirable way.

Take them, digest them, for they will build your faith and usher you in a victorious and successful life God intends you to have.

Daily Encounter With Jesus is not intended to limit you in your Bible reading. Apart from what is in here, take time to read more of the Bible. I suggest that you read twenty verses daily, ten from the Old Testament, beginning with the book of Genesis, and ten from the New Testament, beginning with the gospel according to Mathew.

It's my prayer that you enjoy these devotions. In addition, you will benefit more by reading, reflecting and acting on the word of God. The impact that these devotions will make in your spiritual journey will be evident to all those around you. Consequently, your life will be a light to those living in darkness.

FIRST WEEK

THE FEAR OF THE LORD

That men may know wisdom and instruction . . . in wise dealing, righteousness, justice, and equity; that prudence may be given to the simple, knowledge and direction to the youth—the wise man may also hear and increase in learning, and the man of understanding acquire skill, to understand a proverb and a figure, the words of the wise and their riddles. The fear of the Lord is the beginning of knowledge; fools despise wisdom and instruction. (Proverbs 1:2-7)

What does it mean to have the fear of the Lord? The fear of the Lord is not like the fear of serpents and scorpions or anything else that can harm or hurt a human being. While the fear of these other things cause us to keep away from them, the fear of the Lord draws us closer to Him. To fear the Lord means to hate sin and evil and to walk in His ways. It means to trust and give Him reverence.

There are great benefits when we walk in the fear of the Lord. When we walk in the fear of the Lord, we will begin to trust Him in every area of our lives.

In life, we all face problems, trials and hardships. We all face uncertainties. But in those hard times, 'TRUST' will always confess, *"I know the Lord will make a way for me, I know He cannot fail or forsake me."*

When we begin to trust the Lord, we will cease to worry and peace will begin to reign in our hearts despite difficulties around us.

People get sicknesses like high blood pressure, ulcers, headaches among others because of worry and fear. Trust in the Lord will keep us in good health.

It is possible for us to live in this world of troubles without fear and anxiety. Rejecting fear and worry will solve all our problems because God works for those who put their trust in Him.

Trust will also help us not to compromise our faith. Because of trust, we will always have a positive confession on our lips and we will walk in victory and have good health.

If you have been living a life of worry and anxiety, make a decision today to say bye to fear and worry. Begin to trust the Lord in every area of your life and you will be amazed at the things the Lord will do for you.

THE FEAR OF THE LORD

The fear of the Lord is the beginning of knowledge; fools despise wisdom and instruction. Hear, my son, your father's instruction, and reject not your mother's teaching; for they are a fair garland for your head, and pendants for your neck. My son; if sinners entice you, do not consent. If they say, "come with us, let us lie in wait for blood, let us wantonly ambush the innocent; like Sheol let us swallow them alive and whole, like those who go down to the pit; . . ."(Proverbs 1:7-12)

Those who fear the Lord love to do what pleases Him. They hate what He hates because they want to live lives that are pleasing to Him.

A young man who walks in the fear of the Lord will not walk in the company of those who argue that boyfriend girlfriend sexual relationship is okay because we are living in modern days. He/she will know that the same word of God which is ancient is also modern, it speaks to all generations at all times because it is the same yesterday, today and forever.

A wife who fears the Lord will not strive to be the head of the family or be disrespectful to her husband. A son or daughter who fears the Lord will honour and respect his/her parents. A pastor who fears the Lord will serve the people God has entrusted to him as someone who will give an account to God. And also the sheep who fear the Lord will honour and submit to the pastor as God's servant.

Generally speaking, where the fear of the Lord is, people will get wisdom and understanding. These will cause them to do right and live lives that are pleasing to God in every aspect and the Lord will bless and reward them accordingly.

If you want to have knowledge and Wisdom in all your dealings, you need to start walking in the fear of the Lord. It pays greatly to walk in the fear of the Lord.

WHEN MISUNDERSTOOD

Now the birth of Jesus Christ took place in this way. When his mother Mary had been betrothed to Joseph, before they came together she was found to be with child of the Holy Spirit; and her husband Joseph, being a just man and unwilling to put her to shame, resolved to divorce her quietly. But as he considered this, behold, an angel of the Lord appeared to him in a dream saying, "Joseph, son of David, do not fear to take Mary your wife, for that which is conceived in her is of the Holy Spirit; she will bear a son, and you shall call his name Jesus, for he will save his people from their sins . . . ."
(Mathew 1:18-23)

Mary was found to be pregnant when she was engaged to Joseph. Customary, it was such a shameful thing for an unmarried woman to become pregnant.

Joseph must have been so disappointed with Mary. He did not need to ask her for an explanation of what had happened, he just resolved to put the relationship to an end quietly.

Although Mary had not committed any sin, she was misunderstood by her fiancé and other people because of her condition. They took her to be an immoral woman. Well, Mary knew she was clean but she could definitely not explain her condition. It was supernatural. And even if she had tried to explain, who would have believed her anyway?

Have you ever been in a situation whereby your words and actions are misunderstood by those around you and yet you know you are doing the right thing? Whereby you say or do something to help someone but instead he/she misunderstands your intentions?

Have you ever tried to live for God and people misunderstand you? How many times have you been misunderstood by your husband, wife or brethren? And what do you do when misunderstood?

There is something we can learn from Mary. When misunderstood, Mary did not start running around, trying to explain to every body what had happened in self defense from those who had misunderstood her. Or start complaining, blaming others, no! Instead she left the matter in God's hands. Her condition was by God's supernatural act and she trusted Him to reveal it to those concerned.

Hence, when misunderstood, we too should not to be reactive or defensive but put all in prayer and trust that God will sort out the issue rightly and accordingly.

LEARN TO LEAVE MATTERS IN
THE HANDS OF GOD

Now the birth of Jesus Christ took place in this way. When his mother Mary had been betrothed to Joseph, before they came together she was found to be with child of the Holy Spirit; and her husband Joseph, being a just man and unwilling to put her to shame, resolved to divorce her quietly. But as he considered this, behold, an angel of the Lord appeared to him in a dream saying, "Joseph, son of David, do not fear to take Mary your wife, for that which is conceived in her is of the Holy Spirit; she will bear a son, and you shall call his name Jesus, for he will save his people from their sins . . . ."
(Mathew 1:18-23)

Many Christians, in contrast to Mary's reaction when misunderstood waste a lot of time and energy trying to explain things they are not able to explain and convince people about. But in most cases, such efforts end up being unfruitful, thus they end up being frustrated.

When Mary left the matter in God's hands, the Lord showed Joseph her situation. So as he was considering putting the relationship to an end, the Lord sent His angel to him and told him to continue with the relationship with Mary. Only God could convince Joseph that Mary was not an immoral woman.

There is something good about Joseph's reaction that we should take. Although he was considering ending the relationship with Mary because he thought she had been unfaithful, he was intending to do it quietly. Joseph had no intention of exposing his fiancé Mary.

We need to act like Joseph when we don't understand our brethren's actions. If we feel we cannot continue running a business with a brother because we are suspicious of his dealings, we will do well if we do it quietly. We don't need to go around telling everybody what we think the brother is doing wrong.

When we are misunderstood, we need to learn to leave the matter in God's hands. He knows how to sort out issues perfectly well.

Wednesday

Morning Devotion

ARE YOU WHERE GOD WANTS YOU TO BE, DOING WHAT HE WANTS YOU TO DO?

Paul, an apostle of Jesus Christ by the will of God, To the saints who are also faithful in Christ Jesus: Grace to you and peace from God our father and the Lord Jesus Christ."(Ephesians 1:1-2)

Paul begins his letter by introducing himself as an apostle of Jesus Christ by the will of God. In other words, Paul was saying that he knew who he was and what God wanted him to do. He knew that God's will for him was to be an apostle.

So being in the apostolic ministry was not Paul's decision. It was not by the will of man either but by the will and plan of God.

As with Paul, God has a plan and a purpose for every child of His. So as Christians, we need to know as to where we are and as to whether what we are doing is in God's plan for our lives. We should not go to places and do certain things because others doing them. We need to take time before God and find out His specific plan and purpose for our lives.

We need to understand that fulfillment, contentment and success in life come by discovering and doing the will of God for our lives.

There is a geographical location where God wants you to be, there is a specific job where He wants to bless you and there is a specific person He wants you to get married to. In other words, God has a specific plan for each of us and we need to get it from Him.

It is worth taking time to find God's will for our lives and doing it because it is by being in God's will in every area of life that we will be fulfilled and contented in life.

HOW TO KNOW GOD'S SPECIFIC WILL FOR OUR LIVES

"Paul, an apostle of Christ Jesus by the will of God, to the saints who are also faithful in Christ Jesus: Grace to you and peace from God our father and the Lord Jesus Christ."(Ephesians 1:1-2)

The Bible does not tell us whom to marry, where to live, which job to do. So how do we know God's specific will for us? People may ask.

When it comes to such issues which are not specified in God's word, we should follow joy and peace in our hearts, and if we do so, we will not go wrong. *"For you shall go out in joy, and be led forth in peace . . ."* (Isaiah 55:12). For instance, if you are doing or considering doing something but then you lose peace about it, then you should know that is not God's will for you. You should then stop doing it and if it is something you are planning to do, it will be wise of you to cancel out that plan.

One servant of God put it this way, *"If basically, primarily, most of the time you are frustrated in your situation, you lack joy and peace, then you are not in God's will. Lack of joy and peace, difficulty means there is no grace to perform or to be in a situation or a place. Ease, joy, peace means there is grace to perform or to be in the situation, so it is God's will. Difficult and hard times come when we are in God's will but such times cannot be the largest percentage of our time or situation. Those things come in because we are tempted and tried. If your situation is frustrating it cant be of God because God does not lead us into frustration."*

So, if you want to know God's specific will for your life, you need to take plenty of time in prayer, ask the Lord to show you what He wants you to be and what He wants you to do. Look at the things that come with ease to you, things you have peace about. As you seek Him, God will reveal to you His plan and purpose for your life.

WHO IS A BLESSED MAN?

Blessed is the man who walks not in the counsel of the wicked, nor stands in the way of sinners, nor sits in the sit of scoffers; but his delight is in the law of the Lord, and on his law he meditates day and night. He is like a tree planted by streams of water, and yields its fruit in its season, and its leaf does not wither. In all he does, he prospers. The wicked are not so, but are like chaff which the wind drives away . . . . (Psalms 1:1-6)

Many times we pronounce blessings upon each other, *"God bless you brother,"* we say, *"God bless you sister"*, we keep on saying. It's alright to do that but we need to realize that no matter how many blessings are pronounced upon us, if we live in disobedience to God's word, we will not be blessed.

But a man/ woman who will not walk in the way of the wicked and walks in the light of

God's word is blessed whether blessings are pronounced upon him by man or not. God is the source of all blessings and so blessings will only come to us by doing His will.

What does it mean to walk in the counsel of the wicked and sit in the seat of scoffers? It's living the way none believers do, doing the things they do, talking the way they talk and getting wrong counsel from them.

There are some Christians whom we look at and we can tell the difference between them and non believers; their way of life reflects that they are in Christ. But there are other Christians on the other hand who generally do things the way the worldly people do them and it is not easy for those who see them to tell that there is something different about them.

If you are born again, remember God has called you out of the works of darkness to be a light to the world. You are therefore expected to live a life that glorifies God in every respect. If you have a problem you should pray about it and if need be, ask for counsel from the men and women of God and not from those who would advise you to get into wrong ways like consulting witch doctors, astrologers, enchanters and the like; and to involve you in other evils.

If we walk in the light of God's word, we will surely be blessed in all our doing.

WHAT KIND OF THINGS DO WE TAKE DELIGHT IN?

Blessed is the man who walks not in the counsel of the wicked, nor stands in the way of sinners, nor sits in the seat of scoffers; but delight in the law of the Lord, and on his law he meditates day and night. (Psalms 1:1-2)

Things we delight in take much of our time because we enjoy doing them.

There are many different things people take delight in. Some of the things people delight in are good and beneficial to them. However, others are not beneficial at all and some are even very destructive to human life.

Some people delight in watching football and television. There is totally nothing wrong with watching television and football. However if these occupy most of our time and we neglect the necessary and productive things we should do, then we have a problem.

For instance, there are some people who will sit before a television set and watch all the programs up to late hours of the night until the last program is over. Such people can afford to go for days without reading the Bible because they claim to be busy but they will never fail to make time for watching football and television.

We need to consider the things we delight in and ask ourselves as to whether they really benefit our lives in any way. Think of a Christian who takes five hours watching football and then three minutes in reading God's word. We know that Wisdom, understanding, discerning God's will for one's life, which things lead to satisfaction and joy, come by prayer and by reading and meditating on God's word. So why should we spend all our time on things that are not productive to our wellbeing?

So while watching football will not benefit us anything other than entertaining us, being in God's presence, praying and reading His word will benefit us a lot. It will lead us into health and wealth, into Wisdom and knowledge.

A person who reads and meditates on the word is like a tree planted by the waters. The person who does not read God's word is the opposite of this; he is like a tree planted in the desert.

There is definitely a marked difference between the two kinds of trees. A tree planted by the waters is full of sap, full of life and evergreen with plenty of fruit, while the one planted in the desert is ever dry with no fruit, no life and finally it dies out.

Do you want to have a fruitful and productive life? Then stay in God's word. So someone who stays in God's word is blessed because he has life, he bears fruit and is successful in whatever he does because he is planted in the fountain of the living waters, the Lord Jesus.

GOD'S WORD IS A SOLIDFOUNDATION

In the beginning was the word, and the word was with God, and the word was God. He was in the beginning with God; all things were made through him, and without him was not anything made that was made. In him was life, and the life was the light of men.The light shines in the darkness and the darkness has not overcome it. There was a man sent from God, whose name was John. He came for testimony, to bear witness to the light, that all might believe through him. He was not the light but came to bear witness to the light.(John 1:1-8)

Before the creation of the universe, the word of God was in existence. It was there from the beginning, it is here with us now and it will ever be. This word is God, it is Jesus himself. Jesus is the word of God through whom all things were created.

Since the word of God was from the beginning, then it is the foundation of all creation. This word is such a strong foundation; it sustains and holds all things together because every thing created was created through the word.

God's word has power to sustain His creation. The sun, the moon, the stars are upheld by God's word of power; that's the reason they have stayed in their positions through the ages. This word does not only sustain the rest of God's creation but it also sustains and upholds His people. It has the power to uphold the weak and those who are falling. If you feel like you are falling apart, the word has the power to uphold you. It can uphold and sustain us in times of trouble, pain, frustration and disappointment. It is such a solid foundation.

Are you in a deep valley of pain, sorrow, hardship and frustration whereby you feel you cannot make it in life? Has your life come to a stand still whereby you feel you cannot go any further? Are you at the cross roads, in the valley of decision whereby you are about to make a disastrous decision because of your situation?

All you need to do is to go to the word God. The word contains a promise for every situation man can ever face. So take time to find the promise concerning your situation, hold on to it and you will make it.

CHRIST IS THE LIGHT

In him was life, and the life was the light of men. The light shines in the darkness, and the darkness has not overcome it. There was a man sent from God, whose name was John. He came for testimony, to bear witness to the light, that all might believe through him. He was not the light, but came to bear witness to the light.(John 1:4-8)

In Christ, there is life. Without Him man has no life. While the law of life is working in those who know Christ, the law of death is working in those who don't know Him.

The life we have in Christ is light. Remember we are living in a world of sin and darkness. Where sin is, there is darkness and where there is light, there is righteousness and holiness.

Wherever we are as Christians, we should let our light shine to those around us. Our words and actions should reflect the light of Christ in us. Remember wherever we are as Christians, God counts on us to show Christ to the world by letting His light shine through us, because we are the instruments He uses to take the light to His people.

There are people who do not know the right things to do, your right words and conduct will show them the right things to do. There are some out there who will not listen to your words but will keenly watch your actions. And that is why the word of God says that *"Faith without action is dead"*.

So by our actions, we can win many to the Lord Jesus Christ. If we continue doing right, even when it seems to be hard, if we don't compromise our faith, our light will shine through because darkness can never overcome light.

YOU NEED WISDOM

Wisdom cries aloud in the street; in the markets she raises her voice; on the top of the walls she cries out; at the entrance of the gates she speaks: "How long, o simple ones, will you love being simple? How long will scoffers delight in their scoffing and fools hate knowledge? Give heed to my reproof; behold I will pour out my thoughts to you; I will make my thoughts known to you . . ." (Proverbs 1:20-23)

Believers need to have Wisdom. It is such a great treasure the Lord has put at our disposal.

Wisdom will lead us to be wise in the affairs of life. While Wisdom will lead us to be objective in our judgment, lack of Wisdom will cause people to act unreasonably in the affairs of life; in businesses, relationships, in the way they handle finances and in every way.

We may be having a lot of money but if we have no Wisdom, that money will vanish like wind. A man or woman who has no Wisdom will end up a failure in marriage. A wife can fail her own marriage by her foolish words she speaks out of lack of Wisdom. A man can break his own marriage by not showing love to his wife and being unfaithful. Wisdom will teach us how to treat our spouses as we should.

An employer who lacks Wisdom easily treats his/her employees harshly and unfairly. Hence, the business can easily collapse due to discontentment and unhappiness on the part of the employees. A father who lacks Wisdom can lead his own children into rebellion and bad conduct because of the way he treats them. It is only by the Wisdom from above that a parent can know how to raise children in the proper way.

There are consequences of doing things without Wisdom. God wants us to have Wisdom in all our dealings. That's why He tells us in His word that Wisdom is waiting for us at every turn, trying to reach us so we can go for it. He knows we need it. It pays greatly in life to have Wisdom.

Do you want to get on top, to live a happy, prosperous and successful life? Then get Wisdom. It will get you there very fast.

HOW DO I RECEIVE WISDOM?

Wisdom cries aloud in the street, in the market she raises her voice . . . . give heed to my reproof . . . . behold I will pour out my thoughts to you . . . because I have called and you have refused to listen, have stretched out my hand and no one has heeded, and you have ignored my counsel . . . I also will laugh at you calamity; I will mock when panic strikes you like a storm . . . . when distress and anguish come upon you . . . but he who listens to me will dwell secure. (Proverbs 1:20-33)

To receive Wisdom, first of all, we need to read God's word on a daily basis. Secondly we have to confess it. We cannot enjoy the reality of spiritual truth unless we confess it. Man's faith is measured by his confession.

If we are to receive Wisdom, we must confess that Christ is our Wisdom. We should make this confession continually, *I thank you father that you made Jesus Wisdom to me. So I know that today as I walk in fellowship with the word, His Wisdom will be mine at every crisis.'* As we continue to confess Christ as our Wisdom, our conduct will be transformed.

Continual confession of Christ as our Wisdom will give our spirit control over our reasoning faculties, causing us to act in Wisdom from above. Christ will indeed become our Wisdom. And He will guide us on the paths of Wisdom in all our dealings.

Remember, God will always respond to those who act on His word. So begin now to confess Christ as your Wisdom and do it on daily basis. You will be amazed at the results of your confession.

GOD RESPONDS TO US ONLY WHEN WE ACT ON HIS WORD

My son if you receive my words and treasure up my commandments with you, making your ear attentive to wisdom and inclining your ear to understanding; yes, if you cry out for insight and raise your voice for understanding, if you seek it like silver and search for it as for hidden treasures; then you will understand the fear of the Lord and find the knowledge of God. For the Lord gives wisdom . . . . he stores up sound wisdom for the upright . . . . wisdom will come into your heart . . . . (Proverbs 2:1-12)

We should not be only hearers of God's word but also doers. We have to act on it if we are to have results.

Whenever we act on God's word, He has no alternative other than responding to us for He is not a liar. When we act on His word, He does what He says He will do.

We can learn something from the way electricity operates in our homes. It is wired, everything is in perfect condition. All we need to do is to turn the switch; then it will be transmitted so we can use it where we want to use it. So it is in divine life. The ability of God is at our disposal. It is there with us. God's ability is in us but it lies dormant until we act on the word.

As you confess and act on the word, not only concerning Wisdom but in every area of life, your whole life will be transformed by the power of the word. And you will enjoy the blessings and benefits that are only known to those who act on God's word.

WHY IS IT TAKING LONG TO RECEIVE THE ANSWER TO MY PRAYER?

In the days of Herod, king of Judea, there was a priest named Zechariah, of the division of Abijah; and he had a wife of the daughters of Aaron, and her name was Elizabeth. And they were both righteous before God, walking in all the commandments and ordinances of the Lord blameless But they had no child because Elizabeth was barren, and both were advanced in years. (Luke 1:5-7)

Zechariah was God's servant. He and his wife walked in the fear of the Lord. They were blameless before God but they had a problem that was not moving; they were childless. They had definitely prayed for a child for many years until old age but the answer was not coming.

There is something to learn from the life of Elizabeth and Zechariah. Some people think that if you have problems, it is because you are living in sin or disobedience to God. While it is true that some of the problems we get are a result of sin or being out of God's will, we need to under stand that even when we are living right before God, problems will come our way. We get problems because we are tried and tempted. God tries us and Satan tempts us.

In the case of Zechariah and Elizabeth, their problem of being childless was not because they were living sinful lives or being in disobedience. They were childless because it was not yet God's timing for them to have a child.

Like Elizabeth and Zechariah, you might be having a need that has taken a long time and you are wondering as to why God is not meeting the need. Its like God does not answer your prayers and now you are discouraged and feel like giving up.

Be encouraged that God in His time will do it for you if you don't give up. God's timing is always the best. Take the example of Zechariah and Elizabeth. They did not lose their faith in God and in His Time, God met their need.

Is there anything you have prayed for for many years and the answer has not yet manifested?

Follow the example of Elizabeth and Zechariah, do what they did. Continue living for God and serving Him and in due time, your need will be met.

SECOND WEEK

Monday

Morning Devotion

GOD HEARS PRAYER

Now while he was serving before God when his division was on duty, according to the custom of the priesthood, it fell to him by lot to enter the temple of the Lord and burn incense. And the whole multitude of the people were outside at the hour of incense. And there appeared to him an angel of the Lord standing on the right side of the alter of incense. And Zechariah was troubled when he saw him and fear fell upon him. But the angel said to him, "Do not be afraid Zechariah, for your prayer is heard, and your wife Elizabeth will bear you a son and you shall call his name John.
(Luke 1:8-13)

Elizabeth and Zechariah were very old. They must have prayed for a child for many years. If people have been married for a number of years and then they do not have a child, they often begin to pray unceasingly so that God can hear their prayers and grant them their heart's desires.

Elizabeth and Zechariah had prayed for many years but to no avail; they did not have a child still. Their childless state must have caused them a lot of pain, frustration and anxiety. However, they never lost their trust in God, rather they continued living for and serving God in their pain.

When answers to our prayers take long to manifest, we should not stop serving God. Remember our prayers cause cracks in the Jericho wall. We may not see the cracks there and then at the time we are praying, but that does not mean that our prayers are not being effective. And if we do not give up on prayer and trust in God, eventually, on the seventh day, the Jericho wall will get all cracked up and will collapse completely, because it cannot stand the power of our prayers.

You may have prayed for many years for certain things but its like the more you pray, the more the situation gets worse. You simply do not see the answer to your prayers. Now, Elizabeth's and Zachariah's situation got from worse to the worst each day that went by because they were growing older, and in the eyes of man, there was no hope for them of getting a child.

But God had heard every prayer they had prayed, and when the time came for the child to be conceived and be born, God sent His angel to deliver the good news to Zechariah. His wife would conceive and bear a son, thus their heart's desire of many years would be granted because of the power of prayer.

Start believing that God hears your prayers and that in due time, He will send the answer according to your need.

Monday

Evening Devotion

YOUR PRAYER IS HEARD

. . . do not be afraid, Zechariah for your prayer is heard . . . . (Luke 1:13)

There are people who are living for and serving God sincerely but they have got hardships in their lives. They have prayed and done everything they know to do to get solutions to their needs but it's like the heavens are brass above them, the answers to their prayers are not manifesting.

You may be serving God as a preacher, a singer or in some other ministry and you see others getting blessed as you minister to them. Then you wonder why others are being blessed and helped but as for you, nothing seems to be working. You see God using you to help others but your personal needs are not met, your problem is not moving, you are discouraged and at the verge of giving up.

You need to understand that the fact that the answer to your prayers have taken long to manifest does not mean that God has not heard or does not hear your prayers. Take the example of Elizabeth and Zechariah. They had prayed for a child for so long and now there seemed to be no hope for them as they were very old; but one day, when Zechariah was serving in the temple, God sent to him the answer to his need. What had been a problem for so many years was no more. God had been working behind the scene in what seemed to be silent years.

Are you in a situation whereby God seems to be silent? Have the answers to your prayer taken a long time to manifest, and you are wondering as to whether God hears your prayers? Remember God has not forgotten you. He is working behind the scenes to meet your needs. And as you continue serving Him, the answer to your prayers will come in God's own appointed time. This is because God's time is always the best.

POSSESSING WHAT GOD
HAS PROMISED

. . . Moses spoke to all the people of Israel according to all that the Lord had given him in commandment to them . . . Behold I have set the land before you; go in and take possession of the land which the Lord swore to your fathers, to Abraham, to Isaac and to Jacob, to give to them and to their descendants after them. (Deuteronomy 1:1-8)

The children of Israel were on their way to the promised land. God had promised them a land flowing with milk and honey. Notice God does not give bad things, He gives the best; milk and honey.

God has made promises to His children. He has made promises in His word; promises of healing, deliverance, provision and prosperity. He has also given us specific promises individually and all these are good promises.

In *verse 8* of the same chapter, God commanded the Israelites to go and take possession of what He had promised them. So they had to act on God's word according to His promise in order to possess it.

When God makes promises, He sets the things He has promised before us but we have to do the act of possessing. God cannot possess for us, we have to do the possessing ourselves.

And how do we take possession of God's promises? By fighting; We have to fight for what belongs to us, just like the Israelites had to fight and drive out the inhabitants of the land in order to posses it.

We are to fight in prayer and confession of God's word in order to drive Satan out of our inheritance. Prayer is the means God has given us to take possession of our inheritance.

You may be having a promise from God; a promise of salvation of your loved ones, marriage, financial breakthrough, material possessions and others and you are not doing anything about it. Arise in prayer and confession of God's word, drive out the enemy and enter into your inheritance.

OBEY GOD'S COMMAND

Paul, an apostle of Christ Jesus by command of God our saviour and of Christ Jesus our hope, To Timothy my true child in the faith: Grace, mercy and peace from God the father and Christ Jesus our Lord. (1 Timothy 1:1-3)

Paul begins this letter by introducing himself as an apostle of Jesus Christ by the command of God. He was not an apostle by his will or by the will of man but by the will of God. God had commanded him to stand in the apostolic office and he had obeyed.

Paul's ministry as an apostle was not an easy one; he had to face many hardships. There were times he was thrown into prison. He was beaten and rejected by man. At times Paul had to go without food, but in all these, he never turned back from the command of God.

God commands each one of us to do certain things in service to Him. Its important to understand that everything God tells you to do is a command. God never gives you options. So everything He tells you to do is a command because He never makes suggestions to you. He does not need your views or opinions. So in whichever way God speaks to you, whether in a still small voice, or by His authoritative voice, through a dream or vision, know this is a command and you will do well to obey.

It is important to understand that there is always a price to pay for every disobedience to God's commands. On the other hand, obedience results in great blessings. It is a wise man/woman that will choose to obey the Lord no matter the cost because he /she knows that in the end, his/her obedience will end in great blessings.

YOU NEED TO ENDURE WHEN CARRYING OUT GOD'S COMMAND

Paul, an apostle of Christ Jesus by the command of God our saviour and of Christ Jesus our hope. To Timothy my true child in the faith: Grace, mercy, and peace from God the father and Christ Jesus our Lord. (1 Timothy 1:1-3)

In carrying out God's command, things are not going to be easy, just like it wasn't easy for Paul. It is never going to be easy for anyone of us when we are serving God but we need to be assured of one thing that God will always be with us as we do His will.

Through hardship and difficulty, through thick and thin, we still have to move forward because if we turn back on God's command, we will suffer the consequences of disobedience. But when we obey the Lord fully, the blessings we will get in the end will be more than we can contain. And the Lord will also give us the grace to do His will.

Are you in a place where you are trying to run away from God's command because of the trials, temptations and hardships? You better know that you can never succeed in running away from God. But if you put down your signature and determine to do His will no matter what comes your way and no matter the cost, God's grace will carry you through and He will bless you and will also bless others through your obedience.

PROSPERITY IS FOR THE RIGTHOUS

He is like a tree planted by streams of water, that yields fruit in its season, and its leaf does not wither. In all he does, he prospers. The wicked are not so, but are like chaff which the wind drives away . . . . (Psalms 1:3-6)

The word of God says in *verse 3* that the righteous man is like a tree planted by the water side, that yields its fruit in its season, whose leaf does not wither. And that he prospers in everything he does, but the wicked are not so.

The wicked are the opposite of the righteous. That means a wicked man or woman is like a tree planted in the desert. There is a marked difference between a tree planted in the desert and that planted by the waters. While the one planted by the water is full of life and bears plenty of fruit, the one planted in the desert has no sap, no life at all and so, no fruit.

A tree planted by the waters prospers because it has life, and so does a believer in Christ because he has life in him, God being the source of his life. Christ Himself assures us that He is the life as we read from the Gospel according to John.

A Christian should never admire the wicked. A wicked man may seem to be prosperous because of the material things he possesses like land, houses, vehicles and other material things. But actually this is not true prosperity, because true prosperity begins with the prosperity of spirit and soul, by knowing Christ as Lord and saviour. If you are to take a closer look at such a man, you will realize that he is actually a dry tree because he is not feeding from the source of the living waters, who is the Lord Jesus.

But though the righteous may not be having many material possessions, he is actually prosperous. Because his spirit and soul are prospering, if he keeps in God's way, material prosperity will also follow. God will lead and guide him into prosperity in every area of life.

If you do not know Jesus and you are trying to find your way into prosperity, you need to take the first step to prosperity, by coming to the Lord Jesus Christ and He will lead you into abundant prosperity of the spirit, soul and body.

RIGHT COUNSEL COMES FROM THE
GODLY AND NOT THE WICKED

The wicked are not so, but are like chaff which the wind drives away. Therefore the wicked will not stand in the judgment, nor sinners in the congregation of the righteous; for the Lord knows the way of the righteous, but the way of the wicked will perish (Psalms 1:4-6)

It's a pity that some Christians go looking for fruit from dry trees. In case of any problem, the first person they think of getting counsel from is a non believer. And in most cases, the counsel they get from none believers is ungodly.

Many Christians have been mislead into wicked ways by none believers. Men and women who once walked with the Lord are living in immorality, some go to consult witch doctors and mediums because of having taken the counsel of the wicked.

When you have prayed for something for long and the answer does not seem to be manifesting quickly, if you go to seek counsel from the wicked, they will tell you to take the matter in your hands and do something about your situation. They will not encourage you to keep on waiting on the Lord because they don't believe that God answers prayer and some don't even believe that there is a God in heaven who hears and answers the prayers of His people. And so if you take their counsel, you will definitely end in more problems, and not with solutions because Satan has no solutions to your needs and problems.

But a godly man will encourage you to keep praying and trusting God because God never fails those who put their trust in Him. And when you take such godly counsel, it does not matter how long it may take, at the end of the day, you will come out a winner.

If you have been in the habit of seeking counsel from the wicked, you need to retrace your steps and go to the righteous for godly guidance that will bring you results in the end.

GOD KNOWS YOU

. . . . Now the word of the Lord came to me saying, "Before I formed you in the womb, I knew you, and before you were born I consecrated you; I appointed you a prophet to the nations. (Jeremiah 1:1-5)

You need to know that you are not an accident walking on planet Earth, God knows you and He has a plan and purpose for your being here.

There are times when things don't seem to be going right in our lives. At such times, we feel like we are lost among the millions of people on Earth. We feel too small to be known and loved and cared for by such a big God; the creator of the heavens and the Earth so we feel like God does not notice or even care about what is happening in our lives.

Its great encouragement to know that actually, God knows us and that He actually knew us even before we were formed in our mothers wombs.

Before we came into existence, God knew us. He knew how we would look like, He knew the problems we would face and all the needs and cares we would ever have. God knew what would be our strengths and weaknesses. He knew all about us.

There is nothing that happens to a child of God that takes God by surprise. This big God knows the smallest details of our lives and He takes care of all that concerns us.

There are times when you may wonder which way to go. You don't know what to do; you need someone to show you the way. Well, turn to God, He has a plan for your life. Ask Him and He will show you the way to go because He knows all about you. He loves and cares for you.

YOU ARE SET APART

Before I formed you in the womb I knew you; and before you were born I consecrated you; I appointed you a prophet to the nations. (Jeremiah 1:5)

When the Lord called Jeremiah into His service, He told him that He had set him apart before he was born. What did God set Jeremiah apart for? It was for His service, he was to be a prophet to the Nations.

Like the case of Jeremiah, every child of God has been set apart for some specific purpose. God has given us assignments to do here on Earth and at the end of our Earthly journey, we are going to give an account to God of what we will have done with what He has given us to do.

God calls His people to accomplish different tasks. With Jeremiah, his specific call was to be a prophet to the nations. Your call may not be like Jeremiah's, but there is some specific call of God upon your life. Every child of God is called to do something for the expansion of God's kingdom and for the good of others. Some are called to be preachers and ministers in the gospel field; others are given the ability to do other kind of work like running businesses, serving humanity as lawyers, doctors, farmers and in other fields.

As an individual, you need to go before God and find out what He has set you apart to do for that's what you will be accountable for. And that's where you will find fulfillment in life for you can only be fulfilled if you do what you are set apart to do.

Some Christians are very busy doing things God has not commissioned them to do. As a result, they create unnecessary problems for themselves and for others. They are living frustrated lives, busy colliding with others in their God given assignments. To some, such mistakes have even cost them their lives.

If you are not doing what God set you apart to do because you have not bothered to find out from Him or because you fear the task is too heavy, repent, ask Him to show you what Her has called you to do and get to do it, and God will bless and use you to be a blessing to others.

NO EXCUSE

Then I said, "Ah, Lord God! Behold, I do not know how to speak, for I am only a youth" But the Lord God said to me, "Do not say, 'I am only a youth'; for to all to whom I send you; you shall go, and whatever I command you, you shall speak . . .
(Jeremiah 1:6-11)

You have no excuse for not doing what God has called you to do. You need to know that God does not listen to excuses. When He commissions, His commission is sealed. There is no negotiation with Him, no excuse.

When the Lord called and commissioned, Jeremiah, he tried to give excuses. His excuses were that he was young and not able to speak. But God had told him, *"Before I formed you . . . I knew you, I appointed you . . ."* (Jeremiah 1:5)

God was the potter and Jeremiah was the vessel. The potter definitely knew the vessel was able fulfill the purpose for which He had made it.

When a manufacturer; manufactures a commodity, he does it with a specific purpose in mind, so he makes it to suit that purpose. And likewise, when God created us, He fashioned use in a way we can suit the purpose for which He made us.

When God was forming Jeremiah, He formed him for a specific purpose, to make him a prophet to the nations. God therefore knew Jeremiah was able to speak because when He was forming him, He put in him the ability to speak to people.

Jeremiah's second excuse that he was a youth, inexperienced so he was not able to stand before people and speak, but when God was calling him, He was aware that he was a youth and He knew he could make it as a youth.

God calls people of all ages, from all walks of life, He calls the young and the old alike and He equips them for His service. Because God equips those He calls to serve Him, He expects them to obey Him and fulfill their calling. But some people are always giving Him many excuses as to why they can't do what He has called them to do.

Are you one of those who are giving God excuses as to why you are not able to serve Him because of some certain reasons? You better know that God does not accept excuses, just surrender to Him for He is the potter and you are the clay. Allow Him to use you for the glory of His name.

NO EXCUSE

Then I said, "Ah, Lord God! Behold, I do not know how to speak, for I am only a youth." But the Lord God said to me, "Do not say, "I am only a youth; for to all to whom I send you, you shall go, and what ever I command you, you shall speak. Be not afraid of them, for I am with you to deliver you, says the Lord" .... (Jeremiah 1:6-12)

Many Christians respond to God's call like how Jeremiah did when God calls them into His service. Their excuse is that they are not able to do what God has called them to do.

But you have to understand that God cannot tell you to do something He knows you are not able to do. He created you; He knows your strengths and weaknesses. So He knows what you are able to do and what you are not able to do.

Take an example of a parent. There is no sound parent who can put a sack of sugar on the head of a three year old child to carry. He knows the child is not able to carry such weight.

Likewise, God cannot give you a task He knows you are not able to carry out. He gives you the exact measure you can carry and He also gives you the grace to carry it. God gives grace for every task He gives us to do and He also works with us to do the task as He told Jeremiah, "*. . . for I am with you . . .*" (Jeremiah1: 8).

Some people give God the excuse of having no time. They are too busy doing their own things. You need to realize that time belongs to God and that if He decided to stop your clock now, you would not be able to attend to your businesses.

People have all the time to cook and eat 3 meals a day, they have time to chat with friends for 5 hours, they watch football and television for 4 hours but they have no time to visit that sick person, to go for choir rehearsals, no time read the Bible and pray, no time for God at all.

Remember God does not accept excuses and if you don't obey and serve Him, soon or later, you will face the consequences of disobedience.

GOD'S PEOPLE DO NOT KNOW HIM

.... Hear, o heavens, and give ear, o earth; for the Lord has spoken: "Sons have I reared and brought up, but they have rebelled against me. The ox knows its owner, and the ass its master's crib; but Israel does not know, my people does not understand" (Isaiah 1:1-3)

Some people who read today's devotion are parents. If you are not a parent now, you may become one in future. A parent knows how painful and heart rending it is when a son or daughter becomes rebellious. The rebellion of a child will cause concern in a parent.

In the same way, God gets concerned when His children rebel against Him. God out of concern calls heaven and Earth to witness what was happening because it was unheard of. The sons He had borne and brought up had become rebellious to Him.

The rebellion of a child really treats a parent bad. When you get a child, your heart is filled with joy as you look at the fruit of your womb. At the tender age, you give your little one all the care and attention he/she needs, you treat him/her with compassion and love. Your baby is so precious in that at his/her cry, your heart bleeds.

In case of sickness of their children, I have heard parents saying that they wished they were the ones in pain and not their little ones. What touches a child pricks the heart of the parent.

A parent makes plans for the child as he grows up. Some parents work so hard to make sure their children get the best in life.

But after you have done your best and your son/daughter becomes rebellious, disregarding, despising you, it can become such a heart rending situation.

God gets concerned when his children He has borne and done a lot for, having saved, healed and provided for disregard his laws and become rebellious.

If you are living in rebellion, stop and think of your father's love, then turn back into the position of an obedient son that pleases the father.

DO YOU KNOW YOUR MASTER?

The ox knows its owner, and the ass its master's crib; but Israel does not . . . .
(Isaiah 1:3)

There are some Christians who are living in rebellion. They say they know God but their actions show that they actually do not know Him.

Verse 3 says that the ox knows its master and the ass its masters crib, but Israel did not know her master. It is so surprising that an animal can know its master but a human being does not know his master, his creator and God. A human being is expected to have more sense and understanding than an animal.

My father used to keep cattle, and for long, I never realized that the cows knew him, not until shortly after his death. During his last years on earth, dad used to sit in front of our house most of the time. He would sit there and listen to the news and he would have most of his meals there. When visitors would come home, he would always be the first to welcome them.

Whenever we wanted to talk to dad, we always knew where to find him. I never thought that the cows also noted where he used to sit. But a few days before he passed away, he was rushed to the hospital in a comma. While in hospital, the cows would go to the part of the farm facing the direction where dad used to sit and would start mowing the whole day, they would not feed. They sensed their master was missing and so they were unsettled.

This taught me something. I learnt that if animals can sense and know their master, much more should I know my master, the Lord Jesus Christ and do what He wants me to do. If I can always desire His closeness, whereby I can always sense His presence, then I will be the happiest person on Earth. It is my prayer for you too that you may desire to ever live in the sweetness of His presence.

WHAT DOES IT MEAN TO KNOW THE LORD

. . . . but Israel does not know . . . . Ah, a sinful nation . . . a people laden with iniquity, offspring of evildoers, sons who deal corruptly! They have forsaken the Lord . . . .
(Isaiah 1:3-14)

To know the Lord means to hate sin and to obey His word. A person who claims to be born again should hate sin as God hates it.

In verse 3, God says His people did not know Him and then in verse 4, He pointed out the sins Israel was committing. His people had forsaken Him and taken their own ways. And so, for their sin, God had brought judgment upon them.

God has not changed in His dealings with sin for He hates evil and He will always judge sin and sinners if they do not repent.

We are living in a world where evil is on the extreme. As Christians, we are to live lives that are different from that of the worldly people. If we tell the world that we know God and yet we are doing the same things non believers do, we will be contradicting ourselves and we wont help them in any way to change their ways.

If you know God, your life must be different from the lives of those who do not know Him. And when you live a godly life, many will see and know Christ through you.

Remember sin breaks your loving father's heart. He loves you so much; He has saved, healed and provided for you.

Repent of any known sin and come back in fellowship with the father. Then joy, peace and happiness will be yours.

THIRD WEEK

GOD KNOWS YOUR THOUGHTS
AND ACTIONS

But as he considered this, behold, an angel of the Lord appeared to him in a dream, saying "Joseph, son of David, do not fear to take Mary your wife, for that which is conceived in her is of the Holy Spirit; she will bear a son, and you shall call his name Jesus, for he will save his people from their sins. (Mathew 1:20-21)

As Joseph was considering ending his relationship with Mary because she was pregnant, God knew his thoughts. No man knew what was in his heart, not even his fiancé but God knew. Joseph could hide his intentions of ending the relationship with Mary from her, but he could not hide them from God.

There is nothing you can hide from God because He is all knowing. God knew Joseph's plan to divorce Mary because he thought she had been unfaithful to him. He also knew the plan was not justified because Mary had not committed any sin as Joseph had thought, so God intervened and commanded Joseph not to divorce her.

Many times people harbor evil thoughts and plans; they think no one knows what is in their hearts. But God knows all that goes on in the hearts of men. He knows every plan and every intention and He deals with us accordingly.

God also knows all our actions, even those things done in the darkest night. I once heard about one man who wanted to steal some property. Before he did, he looked right and left, in front and behind to make sure he was safe.

But before he picked the property, his little boy said something that opened his eyes to see that there was an all seeing eye that he could not hide from. The boy said, 'Dad, you have looked right and left, in front and behind but you have not looked up.' Those words caused the man to change his mind so that he did not steal the property.

In whatever we think or do, we need to remember that God knows our every thought and sees all our actions, and that He will deal with us accordingly, for He is a just judge. If our thoughts and actions are sinful, we will reap evil from them. On the other hand, if our thoughts and actions are right, we will reap goodness from them.

GOD FULFILS HIS WORD

. . . . she will bear a son, and you shall call his name Jesus, for he will save his people from their sins" All this took place to fulfill what the Lord had spoken by the prophet:" Behold a virgin shall conceive and bear a son, and his name shall be called Emmanuel" which means, God with us. (Mathew 1:21-24)

God had given a prophecy by the lips of His servants, the prophets concerning the birth of Christ. But many years had passed by before the prophecy was fulfilled.

Through the years, many must have thought that God had forgotten His promise. Others thought this was a word of some dreamer which would never come to pass. How could a virgin conceive? This was naturally speaking impossible. But time came whereby God's word was fulfilled.

When God speaks a word, He fulfils it. God is not man that He should lie or turn back on His word. Even those things that seem impossible to man, God will do them for what is impossible with man is possible with God.

God makes promises to us. Some of the things He tells us seem impossible naturally speaking. But we need to believe that God is able to fulfill every promise He makes. It does not matter how long it may take, God will do whatever He has said He will do. He is ever mindful of His word and promises.

Some of you reading this devotion have promises from God that humanly speaking seem to be taking so long to be fulfilled. Be encouraged that God is not void of power and that there is no power in Heaven or Earth or under the Earth that can hinder Him from fulfilling His promise to you. Just hold on in faith to the promise and in due time, God will fulfill it.

IN THE BEGINNING GOD CREATED THE HEAVENS AND THE EARTH

In the beginning God created the heavens and the Earth . . . . and God said, "Let there be . . ."; and there was . . . . (Genesis 1:1-25)

In the beginning, God created the Heavens and the Earth. What material did He use for His creation? His word; God created the universe by His word of power. That means the word of God has power to bring things into existence.

The word of God is the foundation on which the universe stands. That means when the universe is no more, God's word will still be there, it will abide forever.

In creating the universe, God just spoke the word, He said, *"Let there be . . ."* and it was, things came into existence. And after creating the universe, God created man in His image.

Because we are created in God's image, we can also create with words just like He did. And because there is power in our words, we should be careful about the words we speak. Watch your words in every kind of speech, whether you are talking about yourself or others; it could be your children, relatives, spouses among others, for whatever you speak, good or bad, it will come to pass.

It is therefore great wisdom to make positive confessions about things you want to happen to you and your loved ones.

Some reading this devotion are in problems today because of the negative words they have been speaking over their lives and circumstances. If you have created negative circumstances in any area of your life by speaking negative words, you can undo them by repenting for having misused your tongue and beginning to confess positively about your life and situations.

YOU ARE CREATED IN GOD'S IMAGE

Then God said, "Let us make man in our image, after our likeness; and let them have dominion . . . ." So God created man in his own image, in the image of God he created him; male and female he created them . . . . (Genesis 1:26-31)

After creating the universe and all in it, God created man in His image. Of all God's creation, only man is created in the image of God. That places great value on him.

You are created in God's image and you are of great value, therefore you should never abase yourself by doing things that are befitting animals and not human beings.

Our God is a holy God and so being created in His image, we should strive to be holy like Him so we can reflect His nature to the world.

After creating man, God gave him dominion over the rest of His creation. We have been given dominion over God's creation and power over circumstances. That means you can stand in your God given position and command situations and circumstances to be the way they should be. If you speak words over circumstances in faith, whatever you say it will come to pass.

After completing His creation, God saw that everything He had made was good. God does not make or give bad things. We therefore should appreciate Him for His wonderful creation and for the way He has created us in particular.

Some people look at themselves in the mirror and think they are ugly; there is nothing good about them. That kind of attitude about yourself is wrong. Understand that you are wonderfully and fearfully made by the creator of the universe and then begin to appreciate and have a positive attitude on what God has made. It is worth giving thanks daily to our God who has created us so wonderfully and in His own image.

DOUBT IS SIN

And Zechariah said to the angel, "How shall I know this? For I am an old man, and my wife is advanced in years." And the angel answered him, "I am Gabriel, who stand in the presence of God; and I was sent to speak to you, and to bring you this good news. And behold, you will be silent and unable to speak until the day that these things come to pass, because you did not believe my words, which will be fulfilled in their time." . . . and when he came out, he could not speak . . . . (Luke 1:18-23)

God sent His angel to Zechariah with the good news that his wife was going to bear him a son. But because Zechariah and his wife had prayed for so long and now were very old, Zechariah doubted the word of God. He looked at his circumstances with the natural eye and concluded it was impossible for him and his wife to have a child.

Naturally speaking, it was impossible for them to have a child as they were very old. But you need to understand that God does not work according to the natural possibility. Where God needs to move supernaturally, He does. He is the maker of nature and He always breaks the laws of nature where need be.

Because of unbelief, Zechariah was made dumb and he stayed that way until after the birth of the child. His sin of doubt caused him this problem.

Unbelief causes problems, it causes us to lose God's blessings. For instance; because of unbelief, the children of Israel could not enter the promised land.

You need to do away with unbelief because it will cause you to lose God's blessings. If God has given you a promise and you are doubting His word because of your circumstances and the seeming impossibility of the fulfillment of the promise, repent and believe, then you will see God's promise come to pass in your life.

GOD HATES REBELLION

Ah, a sinful nation, a people laden with iniquity, offspring of evildoers, sons who deal corruptly! They have forsaken the Lord, they have despised the Holy one of Israel, they are utterly estranged. Why will you still be smitten, that you continue to rebel? The whole head is sick, and the whole heart is faint. From the sole of the foot, even to the head, there is no soundness in it . . . . (Isaiah 1:4-6)

God had brought up Israel as His beloved son. He had loved him so much but Israel had become rebellious. Rebellion caused God to abhor Israel and this caused them problems as they had calamities upon calamities; their cities were burned, strangers took their land and they faced many other problems.

Rebellion against God causes us problems. This is not to say that all the problems we get are caused by rebellion, because even when we are living in obedience to God, we will get problems because we are tested and tried. But on the other hand, there are many problems which come to God's people because of rebellion and disobedience.

Whenever you get a problem, before you start binding demons, you need first to sit down and examine your life to see if you have caused the problem yourself. And if so, you need to put things right before God and do the right thing that you should do and the problem will be solved. But if your problem is a result of Satan's attack on your life, then you can stand in prayer and confess the Word and you will have the problem solved.

REBELLION AND SIN CAUSES GOD TO TURN HIS BACK ON HIS PEOPLE

"When you come to appear before me, who requires of you this trampling of my courts? Bring no more vain offerings; incense is an abomination to me . . . I cannot endure iniquity and solemn assembly. Your new moon and your appointed feasts my soul hates; . . . when you spread forth your hands, I will hide my eyes from you, even though you make many prayers, I will not listen, your hands are full of blood . . . .
(Isaiah 1:12-20)

Some Christians think that they can continue to rebel against God and live in sin and God will always wink at their sin. They think that by attending church every Sunday and giving offerings, they will appease Him.

You should know that God can never be bribed. You cannot continue living in sin and rebellion and expect God to smile at you. In verse 12-15, God makes it clear that He wont listen to the prayers nor will He accept the offerings of people who continue to do evil.

So you should not attend church and give offerings so as to have God cover your sin because He wont. You should instead attend church services and give your offerings because you love Him and you want to be closer to Him. This attitude results in abundant blessings from God Himself upon your life.

So if you are living in sin, while God's door of mercy is still open for you, you need to come to your senses, repent, believe and ask Him to give you a heart that hates sin and He will hear and answer your prayers.

BE JOYFUL

. . . count it all joy, my brethren, when you meet various trials, for you know that the testing of your faith produces steadfastness. And let steadfastness have its full effect, that you may be perfect and complete, lacking in nothing. (James 1:1-4)

The word of God says to, *". . . Count it all joy . . ."* in times of trials (James 1:2). The time of being tested and tried is definitely not an easy time, but all the same God's word says we should be joyful in such times.

As long as we are on planet Earth, we are not going to escape trials and temptations. These come to all of us and they are meant to work for our good, though its difficult to understand this at the time we are being tried and tempted

There is a difference between trials and temptations. It is important that you understand it. God tries us and Satan tempts us. When we are being tried and tested by God, Satan will tempt us so that we can fail the test and sin against God. Tests and trials work for our good because when we have passed them, we come out stronger and better than we were before. Trials and tests make us become what God wants us to be.

Every time you pass a test, you are promoted to a higher level. If you have gone to school, you can remember the times you were tested. The time of being tested was not an easy one but it worked for your good, for every time you passed an examination or test, you were promoted to a higher level, and it really paid for the many hours you spent preparing for and sitting for the test. So it is with spiritual things. Passing God's tests lead to our promotion, to higher levels where God will entrust us with higher positions for His work.

Are you undergoing a test, be joyful and faithful and endure, knowing that on the other side of it, there is promotion awaiting you.

ASK GOD FOR WISDOM

If any of you lacks wisdom, let him ask God, who gives to all men generously and without reproaching, and it will be given him. But let him ask in faith, with no doubting, for he who doubts is like a wave of the sea that is driven and tossed by the wind. For that person must not suppose that a double—minded man, unstable in all his ways, will receive anything from the Lord.(James 1:5-8)

God in His word tells us to ask for Wisdom. God knows we need Wisdom in everything we do, that's why He tells us to ask for it.

Wisdom will teach us a lot of things in life. For instance; she will teach us how to care for our bodies; how to handle our business; how to live with our families and friends and how to go about our work generally. Wisdom will guide us in everything you do.

For instance, Wisdom will tell you not to overwork yourself. Work is good but you also need to rest otherwise you will break down. Wisdom will tell you that you should not live beyond your means. You should not spend more than you earn, otherwise you will soon get into debts.

If are tempted to gossip and talk about others, Wisdom will tell you that you will reap the same if you do it. You will know that if you talk about other people, others will also talk about you. I have been surprised many times to see people complaining about those who have done certain things against them. Nevertheless, those very people are doing to others the very things they are complaining about, and then I begin to wander as to why they cannot see that they are reaping what they are sowing. Such people just lack Wisdom.

Ask God to give you Wisdom in all affairs of life and He will give it to you generously so you can know the right way to conduct your life in every area. Therefore you are encouraged to pray for Wisdom and also to read the Word of God, which is the source of all Wisdom, and Wisdom will come to you.

GOD LAUGHS AT YOUR ENEMIES

Why do nations conspire, and the peoples plot in vain? The kings of the earth set themselves, and the rulers take counsel together, against the Lord and his anointed . . . . He who sits in the heavens laughs; the Lord has them in derision . . . (Psalms 2:1-6)

If you are a child of God, you need to understand that your enemies are God's enemies.

When people turn against you, you do not need to fear because what touches a child of God touches God. There are times when people rise against you when you have not wronged them. In such instances you don't need to worry because God will fight for you.

People can rise against you at your place of work, your neighbors, relatives and even brethren can rise against you. In such instances, you should not go in the flesh and start quarreling and fighting with them. You don't need to use human strength to fight such battles. Your fighting should be on your knees, in prayer, faith and trust in the Lord. And when you fight that way, you will be sure of being on the winning the side.

God in heaven looks down and laughs at your enemies. He sees that they are wasting time because no enemy can ever prevail against the righteous; who walk in the fear of the Lord for God Himself fights their battles.

If you are faced with enemies go to the Lord in prayer; have faith and trust that God is on your side and you will have the victory.

WHEN TROUBLE SORROUNDS YOU

O Lord, how many are my foes! Many are rising against me; many are saying, there is no help for him in God. But thou, o Lord, art a shield about me, my glory, and the lifter of my head. I cry aloud to the Lord and he answers me from his holy hill . . . I am not afraid of ten thousands of people who have set themselves against me round about. Arise, O Lord ! Deliver me, O my God . . . . for thou dost smite all my enemies . . .
(Psalms 3:1-8)

When you have problems and enemies, where do you turn to for help? In times of trouble, when you look at your situation, many times there seem to be no help for you. You turn around and there is no man to help.

But if you know God, you will take Him as your shield and refuge. When God becomes your shield and refuge, though these things may surround you, they will not be able to touch you, they will not touch your heart and they will not touch your faith in God.

Troubles and problems cannot sweep you away because God is a strong wall round about you. That's why in hard times, a believer can still walk with his head up and boldly say
"God is good, God fights my battles, God protects me, I will never fear anything. He is the lifter of my head."

And when God becomes the lifter of your head, you will begin to walk in victory regardless of what happens to you.

SEEK WISDOM

. . . yes, if you cry out for insight and raise your voice for understanding, if you seek it like silver and search for it as for hidden treasures; then you will understand the fear of the Lord and find the knowledge of God. (Proverbs 2: 3-5)

You should seek Wisdom more than you seek money. People spend a lot of time seeking money and working for it. Nevertheless, when they fail to get the money they are seeking, they end up getting frustrated.

Understand that success in every area of life; be it financial, social or spiritual comes by applying Wisdom, not education as some people think. Education is not bad, but it cannot give you Wisdom.

Education is just loading the mind with facts. This is accumulation of knowledge that may be of no value whatsoever. It is a known fact that

80% of the knowledge accumulated in schools, colleges, reading and observation is not used by the average person.

We are not using more than 10% of our abilities and knowledge. Think of a man who knows it is not good to smoke but he smokes just the same. He knows it is not good for his body to stay awake half the night carousing. He knows he is not living up to his knowledge. He knows he should not take certain drinks and eat certain foods. He is not using the knowledge he has and so he lacks Wisdom.

Wisdom is a great treasure. However, it is a pity that many people, even those who call themselves Christians lack it. Hence, you are absolutely encouraged to seek it more than you seek silver and gold. Indeed, you need to take time reading and reflecting God's word especially the book of Proverbs that explicates what Wisdom is and how you can get it.

SEEK WISDOM

. . . . yes, if you cry out for insight . . . if you seek it like silver and search for it as for hidden treasures . . . for the Lord gives wisdom . . . he stores up sound wisdom for the upright . . . for wisdom will come into your heart . . . . (Proverbs 2:3-12)

We need to ask the Lord for Wisdom. God gives Wisdom and knowledge. He has stores of Wisdom.

If a smoker gets Wisdom, he will not pick another cigarette. If a drunkard gets Wisdom, he will come out of the drinking habit.

One servant of God in trying to emphasize the need for Wisdom wrote, "You know you should spend more time in study. You know you should stop wasting your time in foolish conversation and talk and begin to utilize the forces in you and the opportunities you can make for study and mental improvement. The thing you need is

Wisdom. Wisdom is crying at the gate; her voice is heard at the portal of every business house, and men are heedless of her warning. They are not using the gifts God has given them. They are not acting on the knowledge that will make them successful and happy."

A wise man or woman will not ignore Wisdom's cry but will heed it because he/she knows that there are great benefits in applying Wisdom in every area of life.

WHEN YOU GET WISDOM YOU WILL GO OVER THE TOP

. . . for wisdom will come into your heart . . . discretion will watch over you; understanding will guard you . . . . you will be saved from . . . for the upright will inhabit the land, and men of integrity will remain in it . . . . (Proverbs 2:10-22)

Verse 10 reads *". . . for wisdom will come in your heart . . ."* We are not born with Wisdom. Wisdom comes to us at some point in life when we seek and ask the Lord for it. And when it comes into our hearts, we can never be the same again. Our lives are transformed for the best.

In talking about the need for Wisdom, one servant of God said this, "Are you unsatisfied with your salary? Then look into your life. What have you that is worthwhile? Two things are necessary: first, find the gift; second drive yourself to develop the gift until it is of commercial value. Maybe you have a good voice but it is of no value to you. If it were developed and trained; it would bring a splendid income. You are saying, 'I have a good voice. I have natural ability.' But you are not using that gift. When you get the Wisdom and develop the gift, it will benefit you a lot. Maybe you have another gift God has given you, if you use it well, you will inhabit and possess the land, things will go well with you."

It is important that you take time to discover that gift, that potential and ability God has given you. For to every human being God has given a talent to be developed for his/her benefit and that of humanity at large.

Seek Wisdom because it will lead you to prosperity. By Wisdom, you will be able to touch the blessings God has in store for you.

FOURTH WEEK

WISDOM IS AVAILABLE TO EVERY MAN

. . . making your ear attentive to wisdom . . . if you seek it like silver and search for it like for hidden treasures; then you will understand the fear of the Lord . . . for the Lord gives wisdom . . . he stores up sound wisdom for the upright . . . for wisdom will come into your heart . . . So you will walk in the way of good men . . . For the upright will inhabit the land . . . (Proverbs 2:1-22)

I once read an article written by a man of God who said something about Wisdom that has greatly blessed me. This is what he said, *"Wisdom is at the disposal of every man. God has given every man ability to accomplish certain things. No man needs to be a failure. People have different abilities. Perhaps you have some ability. It lies there dormant like gold in the stream where a thousand boats have passed over it, and thousands of men and women have bathed in the waters. Beneath their feet was a fortune, but they did not know it. You have seen all this ability in yourself, and you have played with it as carelessly as those swimmers, or as those men and women who are riding over that gold. Wisdom is crying today. She has made her feast, she is inviting you to come and join her, but you persist in rejecting her solicitations and ignoring her warnings."*

It is high time you paid attention to the cry of Wisdom for she will get you on top. It is such a great treasure you cannot afford to miss. You can go for this great treasure God has put at your disposal by spending time in God's word which is the source of Wisdom.

YOU NEED THE BAPTISM OF THE HOLY SPIRIT

. . . And while staying with them he charged them not to depart from Jerusalem, but to wait for the promise of the father, which he said, "you heard from me, for John baptized with water, but before many days you shall be baptized with the Holy Spirit." . . . But you shall receive power when the Holy Spirit has come upon you, and you shall be my witnesses in Jerusalem and in all Judea and Samaria and to the end of the earth" . . . (Acts 1:1-9)

After His resurrection, Jesus appeared to the disciples during the 40 days He was on Earth before He ascended to the father. During that time, He was speaking of the kingdom of heaven.

Jesus had walked with the disciples for 3 years. Now He was about to go back to the father but

He was not going to leave them alone. So He promised to send them the Holy Spirit, thus He charged them to stay in Jerusalem and wait for the Holy Spirit. After receiving the Holy Spirit, they would receive power that would enable them to be His witnesses.

Every believer needs the baptism of the Holy Spirit so that he/she can receive the power to be a witness for Christ. After receiving Christ as your Lord and saviour, you need to have another experience; the baptism of the Holy Spirit.

Without the baptism of the Holy Spirit, the disciples lacked courage to witness for Christ. But when the Holy Spirit came, they got power, they got courage and they became His witnesses.

You are called to be a witness for Christ. You therefore need the baptism of the Holy Spirit as this experience will enable you to witness for Him.

Do you want to be baptized with the Holy Spirit? From the bottom of your heart ask God to baptize you in the name of Jesus and He will.

Tuesday

Morning Devotion

JESUS IS COMING BACK

And when he had said this, as they were looking on, he was lifted up, and a cloud took him out of their sight. And while they were gazing into heaven as he went, two men, stood by them in white robes, and said, "Men of Galilee, why do you stand looking into heaven? This Jesus, who was taken up from you into heaven, will come in the same way as you saw him go into heaven.(Acts 1:9-12)

After having charged the disciples to stay in Jerusalem and wait for the Holy Spirit, Jesus was lifted up to heaven. His disciples saw Him going. It is a fact that Jesus went back to Heaven, the disciples are witnesses to this.

It is also a fact that Jesus is coming back. As the disciples gazed into heaven as Jesus was going, the angels of the Lord told them that Jesus would come back in the same way they saw Him go.

It is many years now since Jesus went to heaven and we have not yet seen the fulfillment of His promise of returning to Earth. And so some people laugh and ridicule when we talk of the second coming of Jesus. They argue that Christians throughout the ages, have been making the same claim but it never comes to pass. They don't believe Jesus will come again.

But the fact is; He is coming back and every eye will see Him. All those who have rejected Him will see Him and for them He will come as a judge. But for those who have accepted Him as their Lord and savior, He will come to reward them.

It is therefore important that you prepare for the coming of the Lord. If you are not born again, it is high time you accepted Jesus as your Lord and saviour so that when He comes He will take you with Him. And if you are born again, you should live your life for Him. You should put away all sin and live a clean and holy life so that when He comes He may find you ready.

GOD HEARS WHEN WE CALL
UPON HIM

Answer me when I call, O God of my right! Thou hast given me room when I was in distress. Be gracious to me, and hear my prayer ... know that the Lord has set apart the godly for himself; the Lord hears when they call upon him. (Psalms 4:1-3)

Our God is a father, He hears the cries of His children and He answers them.

As long as we are on planet Earth, there will always be hard and difficult times. God has not promised us a trouble free life but to be with us always. So whenever we go to Him in prayer in times of need, difficulty and adversity and make our requests known to Him, He will hear us and will provide solutions to our needs.

The writer of this psalm, king David was a man who had many troubles. There were many times in his life whereby he was faced with such adversity where there seemed to be no hope for him. Naturally speaking, it looked like he would be swallowed up by his enemies and adverse situations. But David knew where to run to in such times. He always run to his God and he trusted that He would help him. And indeed, God always made a way for him and delivered him from his troubles.

Just like King David did, you should make it a habit always to go to God in times of need and trouble for He hears us whenever we call upon Him. He hears the faintest cries of His children. He will always make a way for you even where there seem to be no way. So don't hesitate to come to your heavenly father even in the most difficult times of your life, for God loves you and His ears are ever open to your cry.

DON'T BE UNFAITHFUL

How the faithful city has become a harlot, she that was full of justice! Righteousness lodged in her, but now murderers. Your princes are rebels and companions of thieves. Everyone loves a bribe and runs after gifts . . . Therefore the Lord says . . . ." Ah, I will vent my wrath on my enemies . . . I will turn my hand against you . . . (Isaiah 1:21-31)

Israel was once faithful to God, but now she had become unfaithful. She had left God's way and was now walking in her own ways. She had started practicing all kinds of evil; harlotry, murder, bribery and other evils.

It is so surprising that Israel who was once so faithful to her God could backslide to the extent of committing such evils that were practiced by those who did not know God. Israel had drifted away from the God who had loved her so much that He had delivered them from bondage and led them to a land of blessings, a land flowing with milk and honey and had established them there.

Through the generations, God's people continue to become unfaithful to Him. We have always seen Christians who were once committed to God but later turned their backs on Him by walking in evil ways that don't befit God's people. They may not be committing such sins as what man terms as big sins; sins like murder and adultery. But you need to understand that before God, all evil doing is sin. God does not grade sin as man does. If you don't commit adultery but you tell lies, before God, you are as much a sinner as the one who commits adultery. If you don't steal but you gossip, you are as much a sinner as the person who commits murder.

You find believers who once hated evil conversation now delighting in it. They would not sit down to gossip about a brother, they would not hold any evil attitudes, they would never tell lies, but now they don't find any problem in committing such evils. Instead they delight in them. They have become unfaithful to God.

If you have become unfaithful to God, you should know that God is not pleased with your ways. And if you don't amend them, sooner or later, you will encounter God's judgment. So retrace your steps now and come back to your loving father for there is still pardon for you.

THE MOUNTAIN OF THE HOUSE
OF THE LORD

. . .It shall come to pass in the latter days that the mountain of the house of the Lord
Shall be established as the highest of the mountains, and shall be raised above the hills; and all the nations shall flow to it, and many peoples shall come, and say: "Come, let us go to the mountain of the Lord, to the house of the God of Jacob; that he may teach us his ways and that we may walk in his paths." . . . O house of Jacob, come, let us walk in the light of the Lord. (Isaiah 2:1-5)

The Mountain of the House of the Lord is established as the highest of the Mountains. It is raised above all mountains so everyone can see it. No one will have an excuse of not being able to see it.

The wise, those whose eyes are open go there to learn God's ways. And the way to the house of the Lord is open to all those who want to learn God's ways.

There are great benefits for those who walk in God's ways which include life, health, prosperity, protection and the like.

There are only two ways in life that man can follow. You can either walk in God's way which leads to eternal life or in Satan's way which leads to eternal death; there is no middle paths.

If you want to make it to heaven, then you should go to the house of God where you will learn His ways so as to walk on the right paths that will lead you to that everlasting city. That way begins with salvation, then thereafter walking in the light of His word.

Is it your desire to live in eternity with God? Then get going to the house of the Lord for there you will know the way to eternal life.

EVIL CANNOT GO ON FOREVER

For thou hast rejected your people, the house of Jacob, because they are full of diviners . . . and of soothsayers . . . Their land is filled with idols; . . . so man is humbled, and men are brought low . . . the haughty looks of man shall be brought low, and the pride of men shall be humbled . . . for the Lord of hosts has a day against all that is proud and lofty, against all that is lifted up and high . . . in that day men will cast forth their idols . . .(Isaiah 2:6-22)

We are living in a wicked world. Every where we turn, we see evil all around us. Man's ways have become so crooked in that some of the things people do are befitting animals and not human beings.

Some of the things Satan is using to destroy people and especially the youth is pornography and dirty literature. You find a whole generation poisoned and affected by the Spirit of immorality through these dirty avenues that are exposed to the youth.

We need to know that evil invokes the wrath of God upon the evil doers. When people or individuals persist in sin, they will incur God's judgment. Our God is a holy God and so He cannot wink at sin forever.

Over and over, we see God bringing judgment to His people because of sin. God's judgment fell on His people in different forms. Sometimes God would use oppressors to judge His people. At other times, He would use natural calamities like famine and drought, war and exile. God's people had no peace on every turn because God's hand was heavy upon them because of their sin.

There are people today who think they can get away with their sin forever. They persist in doing wrong and they take it lightly, as if God does not observe their conduct. Though it may seem God is silent for a time, a day will come when God will arise in judgment and there will be no escape. If you are living in sin, you better repent and put away sin other than waiting for Gods judgment to fall upon you.

CALL UPON THE LORD

Jabez was more honorable than his brothers; and his mother called his name Jabez, saying "Because I bore him in pain." Jabez called on the God of Israel, saying, "O that thou wouldst bless me and enlarge my boarder, and that thy hand might be with me, and that thou wouldst keep me from harm so that it might not hurt me!" And God granted what he asked. (1Chronicles 4:9-10)

Throughout generations, man has been known to pray to God. In both the Old and New Testaments, we have records of people who called upon the Lord and He answered them.

Some people argue that it is not necessary to pray since God knows all our needs. They argue that God can meet their needs without them having to pray.

It is true that God knows our needs but then you should know that He has also provided the means by which to meet them; that is prayer. You should therefore take all your needs to God in prayer if you are going have God provide for you.

Jabez prayed for 3 things; a blessing, enlargement of his boarder and God's protection. And God answered Jabez's prayer and granted what he had asked for.

The Jabez kind of prayer is a good prayer to pray. You can pray the same prayer, asking God for a blessing, enlargement of your boarders and protection.

If you pray the Jabez kind of prayer, you will be amazed at what God will do. He will bless you in every way; with life, health, He will increase you in your service to Him, financially and materially and He will protect you from all your enemies.

It is important to know that the God of the Bible, the God of Jabez is still in the business of hearing and answering the prayers of His people and He will hear and answer you when you turn to Him.

Friday

Morning Devotion

GOD STIRS UP THE SPIRITS OF MEN
TO DO HIS WILL

In the first year of Cyrus King of Persia, that the word of the Lord by the mouth of Jeremiah might be accomplished, the Lord stirred up the spirit of Cyrus king of Persia so that he made a proclamation throughout all his kingdom and also put it in writing: "Thus says Cyrus king of Persia: The Lord, the God of heaven, has given me all the kingdoms of the earth, and he has charged me to build him a house at Jerusalem, which is in Judah. Whoever is among you of all his people, may his God be with him, and let him go up to Jerusalem, which is in Judah, and rebuild the house of the Lord, the God of Israel-he is the God who is in Jerusalem; . . . . (Ezra 1:1-3)

The Jews had been in captivity for a long time. God had given them a promise to take them back to their homeland after the 70 years of captivity. In His higher ways, God was going to fulfill His promise to them by using means they least expected.

Being in captivity was not a desired experience. They would rather have been in their homeland. They knew God had promised to return them to Jerusalem but they must have looked at the circumstances and wondered how it would happen.

Would God destroy the Nation that was holding them captive like He did to Pharaoh and his men? Would He rain fire from heaven and destroy those who were holding them in captivity? How would it exactly happen? According to their circumstances of being captives and having been in captivity for long, naturally speaking there seemed to be no way out of their captivity.

But in His higher ways, God was going to get them out of captivity because He had promised to do so. God used a way they could not even imagine. He stirred up the spirit of King Cyrus, the very person who was holding them captives to make a declaration concerning their return to Jerusalem.

Cyrus did not know the God of the Jews. He did not even know that there was a God who had promised to take the Jews back to Jerusalem. But when God's time came, He used this King to fulfill His promise to His people.

When God's time comes to fulfill His promise to you, He will stir up the hearts of those He intends to use to work on your behalf. And where need be to stir up circumstances to work for your good; He will stir them so they can work for the fulfillment of His promise to you.

PEOPLE AND THINGS OBEY
GOD'S COMMAND

. . . that the word of the Lord . . . might be accomplished, the Lord stirred up the heart of Cyrus . . . he made a proclamation . . . the God of heaven . . . and he has charged me to build him a house at Jerusalem. Whoever is among you of all his people . . . let him go up to Jerusalem . . . and rebuild the house of the Lord . . . and let each survivor, in whatever place he sojourns, be assisted by the men of his place with silver and gold, with goods and with beasts, besides freewill offerings for the house of God which is in Jerusalem.
(Ezra 1:1-4)

God has a timing for the fulfillment of His promises and when His timing comes, nothing can hinder His purpose.

God can use anybody and anything to fulfill His word and promise to us. I once read a book by a servant of God who had talked of how angels at one time put lots of money in his pockets. He had been praying that God would meet his financial need but he did not know how God would do it as naturally speaking he could not see any possible way of having his need met. God decided to meet his need by using angels.

When time came for God's promise to return the Jews to Jerusalem, He used king Cyrus, a man who did not know God. God stirred up the heart of king Cyrus and he made a proclamation for the return of Jews to Jerusalem.

God can use none believers to work for the good of His people. I once read a book by a certain preacher who wrote of an incident whereby some man called and told him he neither liked him nor the way he was preaching. However, he promised to give him money to support his ministry and this he did.

If God has made a promise to you, you don't need to crack your head, wondering as to how He will fulfill it. He knows exactly what to do for His promise to be fulfilled on your life.

GOD KNOWS HOW TO MEET
OUR NEEDS

Then arose up the heads of the father's' houses of Judah and Benjamin, and the priests and the Levites, everyone whose spirit God had stirred to go up to rebuild the house of the Lord which is in Jerusalem; and all who were about them aided them with vessels of silver, with gold, with goods, with beasts, and with costly wares, besides all that was freely offered. (Ezra 1:5-10)

King Cyrus made a proclamation for the return of the Jews to Jerusalem. Also, the king told the other people to support the Jews by giving them silver and gold, goods, beasts, free will offerings and they did.

It is amazing the way God works to meet the needs of His people. The Jews had been in captivity for many years. Theirs had been a sad situation; they did not have much in the foreign land. But now, all of a sudden, they had silver and gold, goods and beasts. They came out of captivity with wealth.

You may be in a situation that has held you captive for a long time. There are things you need but because you are a captive in some way, you have failed to get your hand on them.

Like He made a way for the Jews out of captivity in such an amazing way, God will make a way for you of getting those things you need even if it means commanding someone to bring them to you. He used King Cyrus to work for the good of His people, He knows whom to use to meet your needs for the betterment of your life and that of others.

YOU ARE HIGHLY FAVOURED

In the sixth month the angel Gabriel was sent from God . . . to a virgin betrothed to . . . Joseph. And the virgin's name was Mary. And he came to her and said, "Hail, O favoured one, the Lord is with you!" . . . And the angel said to her, Do not be afraid, Mary, for you have found favour with God. And behold you will conceive in your womb and bear a son, and you shall call his name Jesus . . . (Luke 1:26-36)

The Lord sent His angel to Mary with the good news that she was to bear the Christ. The angel addressed her as, *"a favoured one"*. She was favored because she was going to bear the son of God.

When God visits you, then you are highly favored. If you are born again, you are highly favored because the Lord visited you on that day you accepted Christ as your Lord and saviour. So you are favored because you bear the son of God in your heart. Therefore you should never take your salvation lightly. And this favour of the gift of salvation is open to whosoever will come to Jesus, and not to some particular people.

When the angel gave Mary the good news about the conception of Christ, she wondered as to how she would conceive since she had no husband. But the angel told her it was going to be by God's supernatural power. Mary then decided to put her reasoning capacity down and chose to believe God's word.

Many times God tells us things that beat our reasoning and we start questioning the possibility of those things coming to pass. For instance, God may promise to give you a car when your salary is not even enough for your daily bread. He may promise you a child when you are approaching 50 and you are not yet married. And then you begin to wonder as to how such promises would be fulfilled because of our human reasoning which is finite. However, God's ways are not man's ways. In His higher ways, He causes what seems impossible with man to become possible.

If God has made a promise to you, all you need to do is to just take Him at His word like Mary did. He will fulfill His promise to you like He did to Mary.

WITH GOD NOTHING IS IMPOSSIBLE

And Mary said to the angel, "How shall this be, since I have no husband?" And the angel said to her, "The Holy Spirit will come upon you, and the power of the most high will overshadow you; therefore the child to be born will be called holy, the son of God. And behold your kinswoman Elizabeth in her old age has also conceived a son, and this is the sixth month with her who was called barren. For with God nothing will be impossible." (Luke 1:34-36)

There is nothing impossible with God. What is impossible with man is possible with God.

God does things that beats man's understanding. Elizabeth, Mary's relative had conceived at an old age, Mary was going to conceive without a husband. These were miracles of God that cannot be understood with the human mind.

God is a miracle worker. He does things that cannot be explained scientifically. For instance, science cannot explain how AIDS and cancer can be healed, but God by His miraculous power heals them.

God has given us minds and we should use them well. But there are times when God tells us to put our reasoning capacity down and just take Him at His word because there are things God does that cannot be understood with the human mind.

For instance, man's mind cannot understand how tumors can disappear by the power of prayer but it happens. Man cannot understand how what man terms as incurable diseases like cancer get healed by the power of prayer but it happens.

Some reading this devotion have problems that seem impossible. Do you have a problem in your life that looks impossible? Begin to believe the Word of God. Believe that with God, nothing is impossible and it will be done.

WORDS SPOKEN OVER A BABY
IN THE WOMB AFFECTS IT

In those days Mary arose and went . . . to a city of Judah, and she entered the house of Zechariah and greeted Elizabeth. And when Elizabeth heard the greeting of Mary, the babe leaped in her womb . . . (Luke 1:39-45)

Be careful about the words you speak over your baby because a baby picks words spoken over it and those words affect it in some way or another later.

When Elizabeth was expecting John, Mary went to visit her. When Mary greeted Elizabeth, the baby in her womb leaped. Mary's words affected the baby in Elizabeth's womb and that was the reason it leaped.

Babies hear words spoken over them, good or bad and they affect them accordingly. If you are a parent, you should be careful of the words you speak over your baby, whether still in the womb or already born.

When some women get pregnancies they have not planned for, they speak negative words about them, some even attempt to carry out abortions; such words and actions deliver to the baby the message that it is unwanted and has not right to live. Such a baby will be born will a spirit of rejection.

Some parents don't even understand that their children have the spirit of rejection because of the words they spoke over them while still in the womb.

If you have spoken negative words upon your baby, you need to undo them by counseling them out then start speaking positive words over them. Speak to them the words of love, life and health and they will become that which you pronounce upon them. This is because what we speak about we bring about.

ABOUT THE AUTHOR

Pastor Adah Nyinomujuni is the founder and president of DAILY WITH JESUS MINISTRIES, a ministry that has touched and transformed the lives of many people.

She is also the pastor of Bethel International Tabernacle, a church where many have been blessed by her teachings.

Pastor Adah Nyinomujuni

Telephone: +255717377746
             +255714963302
             +2557559373927

Email: nyinomujuni@yahoo.com

Daily Encounter With Jesus

We trust that this devotional has blessed you. Please call or send us send us an email on the contacts below and tell us what the Lord has done in your life as a result of reading these devotions. Also let us know if you want to order copies for your friends and loved ones.

Tel: **+255717377746**
       +255759373929

Email: nyinomujuni@yahoo.com

Introducing new books . . . .

1. *Daily Encounter With Jesus-More daily devotions*
2. *How to find your God's appointed mate for marriage*
3. *Various testimonies of people whom God led to their appointed mates*

Watch out for these books which will be out soon